THE PICTURESQUE NATURAL LANDSCAPE OF GUILIN

桂林风光

A PHOTOGRAPHIC COLLECTION OF GUILIN SCENERY BY CELEBRATED PHOTOGRAPHERS

图书在版编目（CIP）数据

桂林风光／谭邵江摄.—桂林：漓江出版社，2007.5
（著名摄影家桂林山水作品精选）
ISBN 978-7-5407-3910-2

Ⅰ.桂…　Ⅱ.谭…　Ⅲ.①风光摄影-中国-现代-摄影
集②桂林市-摄影集Ⅳ.J424

中国版本图书馆CIP数据核字（2007）第063737号

桂 林 风 光

THE PICTURESQUE NATURAL LANDSCAPE OF GUILIN

摄　　　影：谭邵江
责任编辑：廖玉桦
装帧设计：桂林中鼎数码影艺中心
责任校对：秦　灵
责任监印：黎福芝　杨　东

出 版 人：李元君
出版发行：漓江出版社
社　　　址：广西桂林市安新南区356号
邮政编码：541002
电　　　话：(0773)3896171　(010)85893190
传　　　真：(0773)3896172　(010)85800274
E-mail：ljcbs@public.glptt.gx.cn
http://www.Lijiang-pub.com
印　　　刷：深圳市国际彩印有限公司
开　　　本：1/16
印　　　张：3
版　　　次：2007年5月第1版第1次印刷
书　　　号：ISBN 978-7-5407-3910-2
　　　　　　（002000）

象鼻山之晨
Morning Scene of Elephant Hill
象鼻山の朝
상비산의아침
La Colline en trompe d'éléphant au matin
Der Elefanten Rüssel Berg am Morgen
L'alba alla collina della proboscide dell' Elefante
El aurora en la Colina de la Trompa del Elefante

伏波清夏
Fubo Hill in Early Summer
伏波山の夏
복파산의청하

La Colline de Fubo en été
Der Fobo Berg im Sommer
L'estate tresco alla collina Fubo
La Colina de los Rompeolas en verano

独秀峰
Duxiu (Solitary Beauty) Peak
獨秀峰
독수봉

Le Pic de Duxiu
Der Gipfel der Einzigartigen Schöheit
Il picco della bellezza solitaria
La Colina de la Belleza Solitaria

塔 山
Pagoda Hill
塔山
탑산
La Colline de la Pagode
Der Pagode Berg
La primavera alla collina
El paisaje primaveral en la Colina de

尧山之晨
Yao Mountain in the Early Morning Light
堯山の晨
요산의아침
L'aurore à Yaoshan
Der Yao Berg in der Morgendämerung
l'alba alla Montagna Yao
El aurora en la MontaÉa Yao

桂林市景
A View of Guilin City
桂林市の風景
계림시경
Panorama de la ville de Guilin
Blick auf die Stadt Guilin
Il panorama di Guilin
El panorama de la ciudad de Guilin

杉湖日月双塔
Twin Pagodas in Fir Lake
杉湖に建つ日塔と月塔
삼호일월쌍탑
La Pagode du Soleil et la Pagode de la Lune dàns le Lac de Sapin
Die Sonne- und Mondpagoden auf dem Spießtannen See
Pagode gemelle (sole e luna) sul lago dell'Abete
Las Pagodas del Sol y de la Luna en el Lago del Abeto chino

榕湖
The Banyan Lake
榕湖夕暮れ
용호야경
Le Lac de Banian
Der Banyan-Baum See am Abend
Il panorama di notte sul lago
El paisaje nocturno en el Lago del Ficus

奇山秀水
Fantastic Beautiful Hills and Waters
奇山と清き水
기이한 산 수려한 물

Die phantastischen Berge und das klare Wasser
monts étranges et rivières ravissantes
le cime peculiari e la belleza d'acqua
Colinas fantasticas y rio verde

山乡晨曲
Morning Song of the Mountain Village
山村の朝
산가마을의 모닝멜로리

Le matin d'un village montagneux
Bergdorf bei Tagesanbruch
Una canzone di mattina nel villagio sulla montagna
El aurora en la aldea montaÉosa

静静的漓江
Tranquil Lijiang River
漓江の静寂
고요한이강

La Rivière Li dans le calme
Der stille Li-Fluß
Il fiume Li tranquillo
El tranquilo río Li

雾锁群峰
The Hills Enveloped in Mist
霧の中の峰
안개 속 군봉
Les monts enfermés dans les nuages
Vom Nebel verschleierte Gipfel
Picchi coperti dalla nebbia fitta
Las colinas cubiertas por la misteriosa neblina

九马画山
Nine Horses Galloping on Fresco Hill
天然壁絵のようを九馬画山
구마화산
La falaise naturelle à neuf chevaux
Der Gemäldeberg
Nove cavalli dipinti sulla rupe della collina
La Colina de la Pintura de los Nueve Caballos

下龙筏影
Scene of Xialong Bend, Lijiang River
下龍の筏影
뗏목그림자
Die Landschaft von Xialong
Floß am Xialong
I riflèssi di zattere sul fiume Xialong
Paisaje de Xialong

梦幻漓江
Dreamlike Lijiang River
夢幻漓江
몽환이강

La Rivière Li
Der traumhaft schöne Li-Fluß
I paesaggi fantastici sul fiume Li
Las colinas fantásticas cubiertas por la neblina

漓江渔火
Fishing Boats and Lights
漓江の漁火
이강어불
les lampes des pêcheurs sur la Rivière
Fischerlichter auf dem Li-Fluß
La pesca con i cormorani sul fiume Li
La pesca con el cormorán por el Río Li

撒网
Casting a Net
網を打つ
그물치다

Jeter des filets de pêche
Netze auswerfen
La pesca con la rete al mattino
Lanzando la red para pescar

渔樵耕读
A Bookworm Fishman
勤勉の漁師
어부 면학
Das Leben von dem Fischer
pecher · abbatre · labourer · lire
La pesca con i cormorani sul fiume Li
La pesca con el cormorán por el Río Li

竹筏待出
Ready-to-go Bamboo Raft
待出の竹筏
출발전뗏목

Le départ
Bereithalten
Aspettare a pesca
Las balsas de bambú preparadas

漓江之晨
The Lijiang River in the Morning
漓江の朝
이강아침

L'aurore de la Rivière Li
Der Li-Fluß am Morgen
Fiume Li di mattino
El río Li en la madrugada

漓江奇峰
Grotesque Peaks Alongside Lijiang River
漓江の奇峰
이강기봉

Les monts fantastiques
Die bizzaren Gipfel am Li-Fluß
Le colline caratteristiche
Las hermosas colinas a lo largo del río Li

黄布滩　　　　La plage de Huangbutan
Yellow Beach　　Der Gelb-Tuch-Strand
黄布灘　　　　La secca a Huangbu
황보탄　　　　El precipicio de la Colina de la Tela Amarilla

烟雨漓江
Lijiang River in Misty Rain
漓江の煙雨
안개 비 속의 강
La Rivière Li brumeuse
Der Li-Fluß im Nieselregen
Pioggerella leggera e nebbia sul fiume Li
El Río Li en la misteriosa lluvia

金光筏影
Raft Reflection in the Sunlight
光の中の筏
금광아래뗏목그림자

Radeau sous la lumière célestre
Die Widerspiegelung des Floßes bei Tageslicht
I riflessi delle zattere all'aurora
La balsa de bambú luciendo por la luz espléndida

漓江竹筏
Bamboo Raft on the Lijiang River
漓江の竹筏
이강땟목

Radeaux sur la Rivière Li
Bambusfloß auf dem Li-Fluß
Le zattere de pesca sul fiume Li
La balsa de bambú en el Río Li

青山绿水
Green Hills and Clear Water
青い山と緑の川
청산녹수

Les monts verts et les eaux vertes
Grüne Berge und klares Wasser
Colline verdi e acqua trasparènte
Las colinas verdes y el agua transparente

高田风光
The Scenes of Gaotian
高田の風光
고전풍경

Le paysage de Gaotian
Die Landschaft bei Gaotian
I paesaggi di Gaotian villaggio
Paisaje de Gaotian

遇龙河风光
Scenes at Yulong River
遇龍河の風光
위용하경치
Le paysage de la Rivière Yulong
Die Landschaft am Fluß zur Begegnung des Drachen
I paesaggi sul fiume Yulong
El paisaje del Río Yulong

遇龙河之晨
The scene of the Yulong River at dawn
遇りゅう河の朝
우용하의 아침

Der Yulong — Fluss in der Morgentruehe
le martin du fleuve Yulong
il primo mattino di Fiume Yu Long
La mañana en el Rio Yulong

静境生秀韵
Beauty in Quietness
静かな川の調べ
고요함의 아름다움

La beauté dans le calme
In aller Stille entfaltet sich die Schönheit
Le bellezze in tranquillità
La belleza en la tranquilidad

兴坪佳境
Fascinating Scenery of Xingping
仙境のような兴坪
흥평가경
Le site splendide de Xingping
Die schöne Landschaft bei Xingping
La località affascinante a Xingping
El fascinante paisaje de Xingping

漓江夜曲
Evening Scene of Lijiang River
漓江セレナーデ
이강야곡
Le site nocturne sur la Rivière Li
Der Li-Fluß am Abend
La notte sul fiume Li
Paisaje nocturno del Río Li

大地之春　　　Le printemps
Spring Scene　 Frühling auf der Erde
大地の春　　　La primavera
대지의봄　　　El atractivo paisaje primaveral

木山民居
Mushan Residential Area
木山民家
목산거주민
Les habitants de Mushan
Bauernhäuser im Mushan Dorf
L'abitazione di Mushan
La aldea Mushan

小河背风光
Back of Little River
小河背の風光
소하배경치

Le paysage de Xiaohebei
Die Landschaft von Xiaohebei
I paesaggi meravigliosi intorno a Xiaohebei
El paisaje pintoresco de Xiaohebei

光洒千山
The Hills Bathed in Glorious Sunbeams
群峰の光
천산비추는광선

Lumière sur des milliers de montagnes
Gipfelwelt im Glanz
Le colline sotto il sole
Las miles y miles colinas iluminados por el sol

梯田·春魂
Terraces · Spirit of spring
だんだん畑 · 春の魂
다락밭춘혼

Des rizières en terrasse.l'âme du printemps
Die Terrassenfelder im Frühling
I campi a terrazze - l'anima primaverile
El bancal- el espíritu de la primavera

金色家园
A Bumper Harvest
黄金の家園
금색가원

Un pays d'or
Die goldene Heimat
Paese natale di autunno
El paisaje otoÉal de Longji

龙脊风光
Longji Scenery
龍脊の風光
룡길경치
Die Landschaft von Longji
les paysages du village Longji
il terrazzo di Longji
La terraza de Longji

猫儿山
Mao'r Mountain
猫儿山
모얼산
La montagne Mao'rshan
Der Katze-Berg
La montagna di Mao'r
La MontaÉa del Gato

海洋秋色
Autumn Scene of Haiyang
海洋の秋模様
해양의 가을
L'automne pittoresque
Haiyang im Herbst
L'autunno d'oro pittoresco
El paisaje otoñal del pueblo Haiyang

兴安灵渠
Lingqu Canal,Xing'an
興安靈渠
흥안령구
L'ancien canal Lingqu à Xing'an
Der Ling-Kanal in Xing'an
Il canale Lingqu di Xing'an
El antiguo canal Lingqu en Xing'an

全州天湖风光
The Heaven Lake in Quanzhou
全州天湖風光
전주천호경치

Die Landschaft vom Quanzhou Himmelssee
les paysage du Lac Ciel dans le district Quanzhou
Il Lago Cielo di Quan Zhou
El lago Tian Hu de Quanzhou

漓江源
The source of the Lijiang
River
灘江つみなもと
이강의 발원지
Die Quelle des Lijiang –
Flusses
la source de la rivière
Lijiang
Sorgente del Fiume Li
El fuente del Rio Lichiang